BEAUTIFUL GARDENS

THE COLORS OF THE SEASONS

C.R.Gibson®

FINE GIFTS SINCE 1870

Color

How color works to give different
effects has an endless fascination for
people interested in creating beautiful
surroundings. Like all abstract ideas,
color theory is easier to understand
if it is placed in a familiar context.

COLOR WHEEL

❖

Throughout all of our waking hours, we live in a world of color. Indoors and out, color constantly excites our senses. It is not really surprising, then, that color affects not just our view of life but also our moods and feelings. And yet we do not often give very much thought to color: it is so familiar that we take it for granted. We gardeners are very fortunate, I believe, to be more aware of color than most people. How easily we conjure in our mind's eye a cool glade of evergreens or the exact hue of our favorite rose. But to understand a little more about using color in interesting ways to create moods in the garden, we need a rainbow of our own and our own way of viewing it.

THE PRIMARIES

The three primary colors are red, blue, and yellow, arranged at right into a triangle. They are not made by mixing other colors: each one has its particular attributes. We're apt to see red as hot and rich; blue as cool and distant; and yellow as luminous and fresh. While red and yellow abound in the gardener's wheel, blue is not nearly as plentiful (if viewed in relative terms). This natural order of things is just as well, for red, yellow, and blue mixed in equal amounts together make a dark gray of the dullest hue.

THE SECONDARIES

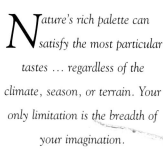

The colors that are the secondaries are named green, orange, violet. These do not exist in their own right, as do the primaries, but are created by mixing pairs of the primary colors in equal amounts. Thus, green is made up from yellow and blue; orange from red and yellow; violet from red and blue. You can see the secondary colors in the picture as three individual triangles arranged around the inner primary triangle: each one spans the pair of primary colors from which it is made. Of the secondaries, green is for us the most important, for it is invariably present in the garden as foliage.

THE TERTIARIES

The primary and secondary colors are placed in the outer ring (*left*, in shadow) where the apex of each of their single triangles touches it. In the space that is left between each of them, you can make the tertiary colors by mixing each closest pair of primary and secondary colors. Thus – red and violet make purple; blue and violet create indigo; blue and green create turquoise; yellow and green make chartreuse; yellow and orange make gold; and red and orange make scarlet. These are all found in the rich world of plants except for blue-green turquoise, which is not a garden color. But, in contrast to the primary and secondary colors, they are much harder to define: no two people will imagine them as exactly the same colors.

Nature's rich palette can satisfy the most particular tastes … regardless of the climate, season, or terrain. Your only limitation is the breadth of your imagination.

Spring

The first bluebells are an amazing
sight. Their clear color mirrors
the color of spring skies, spreading
peace and tranquility over grassy
slopes and wooded valleys through a
veil of dappled sunlight and shade.

PALETTE FOR SPRING

Spring is the time of regeneration, and its palette mingles the joyful colors that proclaim new life. Trees burst into a mass of translucent gold-green leaves. Grass pushes its vivid lime green blades through the bare earth. Daffodils form drifts of limpid yellow. Blossoms mix crisp linen whites with bright ice pinks. Bluebells create lakes of clearest blue. And to intensify these colors, nature adds splashes of orange, scarlet, and cerise.

SPRING SKY WITH JAPANESE CHERRY BLOSSOMS
The quality of light is at its most playful in spring. It tumbles about with renewed clarity as rapid changes of weather introduce intense pale blue and scudding white to the sky. Here, a flowering cherry tree spreads a veil of snowy petals underfoot, and darting shadows illuminate both blossoms and grass.

RED *appears in the palette for spring through a wide spectrum from luminous brights to clear pastels. Blended with the other spring colors, its soft warmth anticipates summer's richness.*

YELLOW *is jubilation in color, breathing life into the reds, blues, whites, and greens of the season's palette. From the palest lemon to zesty vivid orange, yellow has the welcoming feel of a mood that is so well suited to this time of year.*

BLUE, *in all its thrilling tonal variation, echoes the colors of the spring sky and of sparkling water. Set among shimmering new leaves, the calm brilliance of blue shines forth enticingly.*

WHITE *is the color of light and purity – symbolic meanings that make it nature's own fitting choice for the season of renewal and rebirth. Whether snowy or creamy, white adds a spark that illuminates the complete palette.*

GREEN, *in the golden glowing form of fresh young foliage, lies at the foundation of the spring palette, a continuous backdrop that gives a soft clarity to all the other colors of this season.*

Ask of her, the mighty mother: Her reply puts this other Question: What is Spring? – Growth in everything.

Gerard Manley Hopkins

A QUIET CONTRAST

STALWART *PRIMULA VULGARIS*

I FIND THE COMBINATION of yellow, the high-flying color of spring, with purple, lilac, and blue-pink an immensely pleasing one. The contrast is not nearly so strident as when yellow is paired with violet, but the yellow inspires these cool shades of purple and pink and warms them with its sunny breath. Cherry blossoms, hyacinths, azaleas, camellias, rhododendrons, tulips, and primroses *(see left)* all come within this color range, and are enhanced by painterly strokes of pale and gold-green spring foliage.

RELATED COLOR SWATCH

Spring shrubs and bulbs usually flower for rather short periods. A combination that provides for a succession of overlapping colors will make the most of their soft contrasts. Golden forsythia appears at the peak of the season, blooming freely on bare stems. A variegated semievergreen privet gives year-long color, but shows its freshest face in late spring when tender new shoots emerge. The purple heads of ornamental onions and carmine-flushed single tulip 'Renown' fill in the gaps.

ALLIUM AFLATUNENSE
Ornamental onion.
*A bulb flowering in late
spring to early summer.
The heads dry well for
indoor displays.* ●

SWEET SCENTS WITH LAVENDER
*Evergreen rhododendrons have many qualities that recommend
them, not least their bold foliage and fine flowers. Some gild the
lily with blooms that open from distinctively colored buds. The
large primrose yellow trusses of Exbury hybrid Rhododendron
'Crest', pictured here with an azalea, unfold from orange buds.*

LIGUSTRUM OVALIFOLIUM ●
'AUREUM' Golden privet.
*A semievergreen or evergreen
shrub, needing a position in
full sun for its variegated
gold-and-green foliage.*

Single-flowered cherries are, I think, the most beautiful. It's hard to imagine any improvement on this scene of a Yoshino cherry Prunus x yedoensis *spreading a sweet-scented gauze of ice pink blossoms over naturalized 'Fortune' daffodils.*

FORSYTHIA x INTERMEDIA 'SPECTABILIS'. A deciduous shrub of spreading habit. •

*S*pring flowers are ornate showcases for nature's sweetest perfumes.

• *TULIPA 'RENOWN'* Single late. *A reliable late spring or very early summer bulb, supplying in each flower a muted contrast of carmine red and creamy yellow.*

ESSENTIAL SPRING

GOLD, YELLOW, CREAM, AND WHITE: in all their aspects of harmony, clarity, and purity, these are the colors that signal the arrival of spring. Their shining brightness spreads through the land in blossoms and blooms, while trees break into tender new foliage that is an intense lime green. Clearest blue skies, lightly broken by hurrying clouds, smile on this conspiracy of color, giving the yellows and whites even more luminous power and brilliance.

POLYGONATUM COMMUTATUM
Great Solomon's seal. *A leafy perennial bearing demure, bell-shaped white flowers in small clusters during late spring.*

The myriad colors of spring each seem to trumpet the season's rebirth of life.

TULIPA 'OSTARA'
Double late. *A peony-flowered bulb blooming in late spring.*

TULIPA 'GOLDEN APELDOORN'
Darwin hybrid. *A bulb with large single flowers from mid- to late spring.*

RELATED COLOR SWATCH

High spring sunshine bursts forth in this group that combines the rich translucent yellow tones of single 'Golden Apeldoorn' and double 'Ostara' tulips with Great Solomon's seal and the clear, pale green, young leaves of *Euphorbia polychroma*. Broom adds its joyful golden spires and breathes a honeyed scent besides.

CYTISUS x PRAECOX 'ALLGOLD' Common broom. *A deciduous shrub with palest green leaves and masses of golden pealike flowers in late spring.* ●

● *EUPHORBIA POLYCHROMA* Spurge. *A bushy perennial with fresh yellow-green foliage. Loose heads of yellow flowers appear over a long period during the spring months.*

FLOWERY DRIFTS AMONG GRASS
Gold and white 'Fortune' and 'Kilworth' daffodils nod before a fountain of brilliant yellow Forsythia x intermedia; for a softer effect, try F. suspensa. These daffodils naturalize well in grass, if it is left unmown until after their leaves have died down.

A PLANT FOR MOIST PLACES
White skunk cabbage seems an unfortunate name for Lysichiton camtschatcensis, *a beautiful perennial that likes to grow beside, or even with its feet in, water. Its large spathes emerge in spring and stand brilliantly alone before the rich green leaves unfold.*

Summer

In lovely, varied textures and colors
that are vivid, soft, and subtle, a
deep border sings out the glory of the
season. At no other time of year is the
gardener presented with such an
incredible choice of bounteous gifts.

PALETTE FOR SUMMER

S ummer releases an explosion of color in the garden, and gardeners are spoiled for choice. Glorious combinations clamor against lush verdant greens. Contrasts and harmonies sing with myriad voices: demurely in white, cream, lilac, and ice pink; warmly in the sunniest of yellows, oranges, and golds; powerfully in vibrant scarlet and vermilion. And as the season wears on, the song changes to brooding tones of indigo and wine red.

EARLY PROMISE FOR A FEAST OF COLOR
Pale summer morning light illuminates the misty pinks of lilac and ornamental onion heads, leaving blue columbine in partial shade. A softly harmonizing mix emerges among the rich greens of herbaceous foliage, punctuated by darker spires of Irish yew.

• BLUES *in summer's palette often lean toward the red end of the spectrum. This leaning makes them blend especially well with the pinks and paler purples that dominate the early part of the season.*

• YELLOW *has a depth to its rich color tone that reflects the increasing warmth of the sun. All through the season, it's in harmony with orange and golden greens and forms exciting contrasts when used with violet and bluish pinks.*

• ORANGE *is at its freshest and most lively in summer. Lying sociably between red and yellow, it gives a warm and friendly effect in mixes that include these colors. In small quantities with lilac or pink or lime green, its jewel-like quality shines through.*

• PINKS *appear in varying forms from the early peony pastels to the lurid tones of high summer phlox. Then pinks fade in the glow of the first chrysanthemums. All blend happily together with the palette's other colors.*

• REDS *speak with a strong, deep velvety voice during the summer months. Luminous and startling against foliage greens, reds are dulled and forfeit much of their vitality and richness when paired with either blue or violet.*

W*hat is so rare as a day in June?*
    Then, if ever, come perfect days;
Then Heaven tries the earth if it be in tune,
    And over it softly her warm ear lays.

James Russell Lowell

EXUBERANT SUMMER

A VOLUPTUOUS MIX of strong and vibrant colors is a thrilling sight in the garden. Glowing reds, yellows, and oranges encapsulate summer in their rich bold tones. Planted in generous groups to create a landscape of undulating hills and valleys, they brim with a mood of summer plenty, and sit easily beside the cooler purples, blues, and pinks that relieve too strident an effect. This is the sort of planting that will excite your senses, and in sunny heat radiates with the sheer joy of color.

LYSIMACHIA VULGARIS
Yellow loosestrife. A long-flowering, clump-forming perennial that can be invasive. ●

RELATED COLOR SWATCH

When colors of great intensity abound, greens play a major part. They make reds, oranges, and bright pinks leap forward, and take cool colors, in particular blue, into the background. Shades of gold- and lime green, as in bells of Ireland *Molucella laevis*, at far right, bring most colors vitality. Silver-gray and bronze send colors into hazy retreat, and work much better with soft hues.

HEART-WARMING REFRAIN
Mounding orange pot marigolds, lit up by feverfew Tanacetum parthenium 'Aureum' with its white daisy flowers and radiant emerald green foliage, join a rousing chorus in this long border with purple and yellow pansies, red fuchsias, and copper roses.

JOYFUL ABSTRACT
Marvelous painterly effects are achieved with various mound-forming plants placed in blocks of brilliant solid color. In front, at left, rose-pink and crimson zonal geraniums merge into purple-blue Convolvulus mauritanicus. Scarlet poppies and vermilion valerian resound against broad drifts of perennial wallflower Erysimum 'Orange Flame'.

ROSA 'EDEN ROSE'
Hybrid tea. *A deciduous shrub with a profusion of scented flowers from early summer to autumn.*

AGERATUM HOUSTONIANUM 'PINKIE' Floss flower. *Midsummer annual.*

MOLUCELLA LAEVIS Bells of Ireland. *An annual. Its lime green calyces surround tiny scented white flowers.*

CALENDULA OFFICINALIS Pot marigold. *A freely self-seeding annual with a pungent, tangy aroma.*

Summer flowers appear to absorb the bright glow of the sun, capturing its intensity in a way that the unprotected eye cannot otherwise view.

BRIGHT RED DAZZLERS

BOLD AND SASSY, red is the most forward of colors. Placed with green, the color that lies directly opposite it in the color wheel, it's even more so: it seems to leap out at you, almost with a life of its own. I enjoy red most of all used this way. Even if the combination is small scale, for instance plants in a container or a red climber festooned among the luxuriant green foliage of a tree, the effect always elicits an excited response. The strongest impact comes when shades of brilliant red veering somewhat toward orange rather than pink are set against dark glossy greens that resonate with their intensity.

IMPATIENS WALLERIANA BLITZ SERIES Impatiens. *An annual that flowers from early summer to first frost.*

The garden that has been accented with red reveals that the gardener is a hopeless romantic and not timid in the least about sharing their festive outlook with the world.

RELATED COLOR SWATCH

This unsophisticated grouping combines just a pair of plants. They are a perfect choice for a container in a semishaded or even shaded position, and would bring vibrancy to a lackluster corner. Both the fast-growing impatiens (*far left*) and the tuberous begonia provide a lively color contrast from early summer right through to autumn. Scented flowering tobacco *Nicotiana alata* and fuchsias would also suit such a contained planting.

TUBEROUS BEGONIA 'CLIPS'. Excellent for containers, this B. x tuberhybrida (Multiflora group) bears large double flowers on sturdy stems.

DAZZLING CONTRAST
Brilliant scarlet nasturtium Tropaeolum speciosum *clambers up into a dark green yew hedge. It's a real dazzler that needs to be planted about 10in (28cm) deep in rich acid soil with roots in shade and flowers in sun. Once established, it's unstoppable.*

SHOWY CREVICE PLANTING
Give red valerian Centranthus ruber *a rocky crevice in which to grow (particularly near the sea) and it will romp away with abandon. Not so intense a red as some, its massed flower spires still create a fiery show against a strong background of greenery.*

PEACEFUL PASTELS

LAVATERA 'BARNSLEY'

M Y FIRST SIGHT of an early summer alpine meadow was in northern Italy. Its beauty was breathtaking, an impressionistic dream made up of mostly pastel colors. Bringing this vision into the garden is very simple, for these colors, which are full of light, take to each other like rosy-flushed peaches mixed with thick, rich cream. Lemon and apricot; confections in soft rose (the mallow at left) and other quiet pinks; pale lilac, silver-blue, and of course not forgetting white: all or any of them mingle with ease in a picture of great loveliness and unerring quality.

RELATED COLOR SWATCH

A soothing group in which the lilies' stamens provide the strongest color, a bold, zesty orange reverberating against sumptuous hollyhock in an apricot shade that looks rich beside the ice pink lily petals. Here too are lilac statice (easy to grow and ideal for drying), white gooseneck loosestrife spikes, and greenish gold dill.

LYSIMACHIA CLETHROIDES
Gooseneck loosestrife. *A perennial that spreads freely.*

LIMONIUM SINUATUM
Statice. *An open-growing perennial treated as an annual. Seed is available for many single colors.*

A CHEERFUL PATHWAY
Pinks, yellows, and white spill out over a path: their soft colors sit well with the texture of brick. Daisy Erigeron mucronatum, at left, blooms for months, and the abundant honey gold flowers of meadow foam Limnanthes douglassii are rarely far behind.

WATERSIDE CONTEMPLATION
Beside a dark pond, Hosta sieboldiana *proudly flourishes its magnificently corrugated silver-blue leaves. It makes a gentle, meditative composition here in company with pink and white candelabra primrose* Primula pulverulenta *'Bartley', some variegated water irises, and the still water.*

ANETHUM GRAVEOLENS *Dill.
A self-seeding annual. Every part of the plant has a fresh,*
• *aromatic fragrance.*

ALCEA ROSEA
'CHATER'S DOUBLE'
Hollyhock. A rust-free biennial selection in
• *varied colors.*

LILIUM 'LE REVE'
Lily. An oriental lily producing flowers with the most heavenly sweet scent. •

On a hot summer day a fragrant meadow refreshes like a cool breeze.

Autumn

Brilliantly tinted foliage dances along
outstretched branches of Japanese
maples, made all the more gorgeous
by glimpses of contrasting green in the
grass beneath and roughly textured,
lichened bark of adjoining trees.

PALETTE FOR AUTUMN

A month or so before the end of summer a new mood stirs, heralding autumn. Nights are cooler, heavy dews collect, and the garden's color palette begins to change. As autumn gathers pace, sultry tones take over. Oranges, reds, and golden yellows triumph in chrysanthemums and dahlias. Asters amaze in marvelous purples, blues, and mellow pinks. Then flowers give way to glowing berries and the glorious spectacle of autumn leaves.

EVENING IN THE RHYTHM OF LIFE
Decay is more apparent in wild parts of the garden. Leaves turn color and fall, providing nourishment for next year's growth: green is overtaken by gold, rust, and brown. Mists drift in these mornings, especially around water. As the sun breaks through, the garden basks again in warm and honeyed light.

O sun and skies and clouds of June,

And flowers of June together,

Ye cannot rival for one hour

October's bright blue weather.

Helen Hunt Jackson

- YELLOW *reflects the sinking of the sun and remembered summer warmth in many daisy flowers. Later, foliage adds its mellow tones.*

- PINK *reigns strongly at this time of year in dusky hues, and veers toward the soft violets and blues of the color wheel. Their beauty is seen in many sedums, New England asters, and hydrangeas.*

- ORANGE *fits autumn to perfection: it is as if the myriad patchwork of summer color has been heaped on a fire in a burst of flame at the end of the year.*

- RED *is rich and deep in autumn. It is seen in many chrysanthemums and dahlias, as well as the changing leaves of sumacs, cherries, and maples, which glimmer darkly before they fall.*

- SCARLET *puts on a glorious show in holly, bittersweet, viburnum, and pyracantha fruits, which are some of the most vividly colored autumn berries.*

THE SETTING SUN

SYMPATHETIC MARRIAGE

Harmony sits at the heart of autumn in the tawny rusts, rich dark reds, earth browns, and radiant burnt orange that share the hot part of the color wheel. Their closely allied warmth reflects the tones of bonfires and a setting sun, and in the garden they lend a melodious yet fading heat to the year's color parade. Beside autumnal favorites, such as the floribunda roses seen with bronze canna foliage at left, the final glory of summer goes on in begonias, fuchsias, geraniums, and nasturtiums.

DAHLIA Water-lily type. *A tuberous perennial, one of the numerous border hybrids. It will flower until first frost.*

RELATED COLOR SWATCH

A dusky group lit by the candylike orange of red-hot pokers will look especially wondrous as the sun dips to the horizon. This grouping blends chocolate and gold, russet and blood red. It takes us from the sharp, crackling midst of the bonfire to its dark, smoky outer edges that barely catch the dwindling rays of daylight.

COMPOSITION FOR ONE VOICE
All the harmonious colors of the season are captured in a single plant. Shifting from glowing scarlet through dusky orange to old gold, the petals of sneezeweed Helenium autumnale *are set off by large globular pompons of hazy ochre and toasted brown.*

ENDURING MELODY
Chrysanthemums have a pungent scent that echoes their embered hues. These reflexed and pompon cultivars are covered in flower for weeks from late summer until cold weather sets in. Underplanted below, nasturtiums ping against their vivid leaves.

KNIPHOFIA TRIANGULARIS
Red-hot poker. *A perennial with small flower spikes borne on stout stems.* •

LEYCESTERIA FORMOSA
Himalayan honeysuckle. *A deciduous shrub. The white flowers with purple-red bracts produce purplish autumn fruits.* •

CHRYSANTHEMUM *Non-disbudded type. An early autumn perennial bearing sprays of flowers that are* • *ideal for cutting.*

One of Nature's ironies is that a garden's warmest colors blossom as the skies turn grey and cold.

FLICKERING EMBERS

I AM ALWAYS HAPPY to return to one of my favorite color combinations. Pink and orange make such glad companions and are especially cheerful with an injection of pale or golden green. As the season moves on and the garden is readied for winter, it is good to have planned for a farewell vision of animated color. Dahlias, nerines, belladonna lilies, and later-flowering hebes contribute plenty of pinks and oranges to the season's palette. Many roses, too, have flowers and fruits in wondrous shades of these two colors.

RELATED COLOR SWATCH

Rugosa rose hips the size and color of tiny tomatoes, fragile papery ribbed lanterns of *Physalis alkekengi*, and luminous nerines provide elements of brilliant orange in this group for an autumn border. The sugar pink of sweetly fragrant belladonna lilies and rouged carmine of *Hebe* 'La Séduisante' impart a glow of soft warmth.

AMARYLLIS BELLADONNA Belladonna lily. *A bulb producing its flower stems in early autumn after the leaves die down.*

ROSA RUGOSA 'SCABROSA' Species hybrid. *A dense shrub. The large fruits follow a long succession of richly scented, cupped, single pink flowers.*

SPLENDID LATE ARRAY
A deep border can be every bit as delightful in autumn as it is in summer. Fringing and overflowing the lawn's edge are crocosmia, amaranth, penstemon, yarrow, rudbeckia, mallow, dahlia, and rose. All are alive with form, texture, and joyful play of color.

FIREBRAND DISPLAY
Red-hot pokers stand like gleaming torches against a bronze-purple smoke tree and deep pink Joe Pye weed. Pale lemon-green mullein and goat's beard emphasize the zingy clash of orange with pink.

Hebe 'La Seduisante'. A barely hardy evergreen shrub for a sheltered site, with dense flower spikes ● throughout autumn.

Nerine 'Corusca Major'. Plant this bulb in the shelter of a warm sunny wall and protect ● from freezing.

Physalis alkekengi Chinese lantern. A perennial that needs to be controlled. Fruits hide inside ● the lantern calyces.

Autumn subtly beckons the gardener to rest by the hearth where the crackling fire's warm glow captures the season's golden foliage.

Winter

With the landscape of color at its most somber, the pure clean beauty of other detail comes into its own in the outlines of trees, vigorous young shoots, rich evergreens, and flowers that shine like miniature jewels.

PALETTE FOR WINTER

Dominated by the brown of soil, the gray of bark, persistent green foliage, and a sprinkling of berries, winter may seem short on color interest. Yet the garden still has magic. The sharply defined bones of trees and shrubs laid bare produce intricate patterns. Evergreen forms abound in gold, copper, and silver-blue. Camellias and other shrubs grace the view with winter flowers, while crocuses and snowdrops speak sweet messages of spring.

A STUDY IN MINIMALISM

Crisp dried-up hortensia hydrangea heads have a spare beauty, intensified by flooding winter light. The plumed branches, with once-colorful bracts now coated in frost, are reduced to shades of frothy cappuccino. In the foreground at right, a brave little robin broods plumply atop a small evergreen rhododendron.

• GRAY-BROWN *is a bold feature of winter's scene in the form of bare soil, bark, and catkins. Dried leaves, held on hedging plants like hornbeams and beeches, or littering the ground, add a touch of textural interest.*

• WHITE *flowers dominate at this time. Viburnums and heathers (precious spots of light) gleam bright against somber foliage, and survive the chill of winter thanks to their energy-conserving size.*

> C*ome, rich and lovely*
> *Winter's Eve,*
> *That seldom handles gold;*
> *And spread your silver sunsets out,*
> *In glittering fold on fold.*
>
> W. H. Davies

• COPPER, *as tones of red and bronze, appears in the leaves of many plants such as pittosporum, leucothöe, photinia, phormium, and cordyline. Purple varieties extend this color range.*

• SILVER *and biting tones of iron green echo the cold patinas of winter. As with white, they give a brilliant sheen to dreary landscapes. Many conifers, santolinas, and artemisias have useful silver-gray winter foliage.*

• RICH EVERGREENS *have a special value at this time, providing definition for the garden and a suggestion of spring's freshness. Berries are a bonus on small trees and shrubs including holly, skimmia, and firethorn.*

WINTER CHEER

FEMALE *SKIMMIA JAPONICA*

Because of the austerity of the season, when red and green meet in the landscape, the contrast is even more intense than at other times of year. Berries will be the surest source of winter reds, if birds have not taken them all. When planning for them, remember that some plants, including skimmia (*left*), need a male and a female to produce their fruits. Winter shoots can make strong features, too. Willow *Salix alba* 'Britzensis' has a tracery of scarlet young stems that look particularly beautiful near water.

RELATED COLOR SWATCH

This vigorous quartet of plants has color sufficient to brighten the grayest outlook. A glowing collection of stout-hearted spiky holly, dogwood stems, fruiting ivy, and cotoneaster provides an exciting variety of color and texture in its glossy and ribbed evergreen foliage, mahogany winter shoots, and clustered scarlet berries. No less showy, the green ivy fruit ripens to coal black.

SKELETON FRAMEWORK
The whiplike shoots of 'Westonbirt', which is a selection of red-barked dogwood Cornus alba, *stand out boldly against snow-covered ground.* C. stolonifera *'Flaviramea' has lemon shoots in winter. Prune both low in spring to encourage young growth.*

ILEX AQUIFOLIUM
English holly. *An evergreen tree that grows slowly and has many different forms. The fruit is especially profuse after dry summers.*

NATURAL WONDERS
When the garden lacks color, other parts of the scene can fill the gap. The hard-edged blue of a winter sky is nature's own surprise. It makes an incredible backdrop to the brilliant red berries of cranberry bush Viburnum opulus *that follow its lace-cap white flowers and tinted autumn foliage.*

CORNUS ALBA Red-barked dogwood. *A deciduous shrub that has red bark in winter. C. alba 'Elegantissima' has variegated summer foliage.* •

COTONEASTER 'CORNUBIA'. *A semievergreen shrub of arching habit. Clusters of white flowers in early summer are followed by copious quantities of berries.* •

HEDERA HELIX English *ivy. A self-clinging evergreen climber with berries only on older treelike growth.* •

Winter is the season when a garden's colors are displayed inside to enhance the holiday celebrations that close out the year.

MIDWINTER WHITE

SILKY CLEMATIS SEEDHEADS

THE COLOR OF SNOW AND FROST seems particularly right for winter plantings and the mood of quiet watchfulness. When the weather is mild, white brings nostalgia, too, for the crisp beauty of hoarier days. The vagaries of regional climate will dictate the plants you choose. At this time of year, the absence of eye-engaging color lends grasses and seedheads, such as those of clematis (*left*), a unique appeal. For flowers, Christmas roses are the earliest white, followed by snowdrops and – in some areas – white quince and heather.

RELATED COLOR SWATCH

This seasonal planting for a bed against the shelter of a wall will flower in mild midwinter spells through to spring. *Senecio* 'Sunshine' has leaves whose soft felted undersides are echoed in cream-white Christmas rose *Helleborus niger* and heather, opening from pink buds. Flowering quince adds blossoms of spare, pure white.

SENECIO 'SUNSHINE'. *A bushy evergreen shrub with coarse yellow flowers, best kept as a foliage plant.*

AIRS AND GRACES
Pampas grass Cortaderia selloana *needs room to create so rich an effect: plants quickly form massive clumps and are invasive. The fine ivory-colored flower plumes can reach heights of 10ft (3m). They stand all winter, but should be removed in spring.*

LATE WINTER GREETS SPRING
The first snowdrops are a welcome sight, for they seem to say that spring is not far away. Of the many sorts, I think the simple common snowdrop Galanthus nivalis is lovely with its gray-green leaves, especially carpeting the edges of woodland.

CHAENOMELES SPECIOSA
'NIVALIS' Flowering quince.
A deciduous, thorny shrub, excellent for training against a sheltered sunny wall. ●

HELLEBORUS NIGER
Christmas rose. *A clump-forming evergreen perennial with winter to spring flowers. In sheltered sites, blooms* ● *appear in early winter.*

ERICA ERIGENA
Heather. *A tall, slightly hardy evergreen shrub with flowers from early winter until late spring.* ●

*W*inter's white landscape is an opportunity to plan the first colorful brushstroke of spring on your garden's canvas.

C.R.Gibson®
FINE GIFTS SINCE 1870

This book is based on *Malcolm Hillier's Color Garden*,
first published in Great Britain in 1995,
by Dorling Kindersley Limited, London

Developed by Matthew A. Price, Nashville, Tennessee.

Published by C. R. Gibson®
C. R. Gibson® is a registered trademark of Thomas Nelson, Inc.
Norwalk, Connecticut 06856

Printed in Singapore by Star Standard.

ISBN 0–7667–6161–4
UPC 082272–44982–4
GB4138

Picture Credits
Photography by Stephen Hayward and Steven Wooster.

Publisher's Note to Readers
Many of the gardens that were photographed by Steven Wooster for *Malcolm Hillier's Color Garden* will be
found on this page; but where people have asked not to be included, their desire for anonymity has been
respected and their names and the locations of their gardens do not appear. The publisher would be grateful
to be told of unintended errors, omissions, or incorrectly named plants. In the credits, a letter following a page
number shows picture position: t = top; b = bottom; c = center; l = left; r = right.
No letter identifies a full-page picture.

Bodnant Garden 10b; **The Winter Garden at The Cambridge Botanic Gardens** 32 & 33, 36b; **The Beth Chatto Gardens**
13b, 14 & 15, 26b; **Chiffchaffs,** Mr. & Mrs. K.R. Potts 12bl; **Great Dixter,** Christopher Lloyd 21t, 22t, 28t, 29t, 31t;
Hampton Court Gardens 11tr; **Hazelby House,** Prue & Martin Lane-Fox 21b; **Isabella Plantation,** Richmond Park 12t;
Elizabeth Luisetti (New Zealand) 22b; **Matai Moana,** Daphne & Hugh Wilson 19t; **Saling Hall,** Hugh & Judy Johnson
8b; **Kitty & Victor Sunde** (New Zealand) 18b; **Titoki Point** (New Zealand), Gordon & Annette Collier 23t; **Turn Ends**
6 & 7; **Westonbirt Arboretum** 24 & 25